CONTENTS

Preface

At the United States Holocaust Memorial Museum in Washington, D.C., a poignant documentary explores antisemitism and its role in the Holocaust. The film ends with these words:

THIS IS WHERE PREJUDICE CAN LEAD.

That somber warning has guided our work on this series.

The task of creating a series of books on the Holocaust seemed, at first, straightforward enough: We would develop an in-depth account of one of the most complex and compelling periods in human history.

But it quickly became clear to us that, on an emotional level, this series would not be straightforward at all. Indeed, the more work we did, the more we realized just how this subject wraps itself around everyone it touches. As we discussed content with our authors and advisors and began to select photographs and other documents for reproduction, several unanticipated and complicated issues arose.

The first major issue was pivotal, in that our decision would guide the content of the books: How should we choose to define the very term *Holocaust*? Many scholars of the Holocaust believe that the term should be used exclusively in reference to the approximately 6 million European Jews who were murdered by Nazis and their collaborators between 1933 and 1945. This is because no other group was singled out so systematically and relentlessly for genocide. Should the perhaps 4 million non-Jewish victims of the period—the Soviet prisoners of war, Romani (Gypsies), Jehovah's Witnesses, German and Austrian male homosexuals, and other groups—be discussed on the same level as the Jews? Ultimately—in philosophical agreement with the U.S. Holocaust Memorial Museum—we decided to focus our discussion primarily on

the Jews but also to report the experiences of other victims.

Our second major decision had to do with how to present the material. How explicit should the books be in their written descriptions and photographic records of what was done to the victims? Perhaps never before have the brutalities of war and the consequences of prejudice and hatred been so extensively chronicled; perhaps never so eloquently and, at the same time, in such painful detail.

On this issue, we decided we would chronicle what happened, but try not to shock or horrify. Learning about the Holocaust should be disturbing—but there is a delicate line between informative realism and sensationalism. The most brutal accounts and documentation of the Holocaust can be found in many other sources; we believe that in our series, much of this story will be revealed through the powerful and moving images we have selected.

Yet another difficult issue was raised by our educational advisors: Was the Holocaust truly a singular historical event, uniquely qualified for such detailed study as is provided in this series? That it was an extraordinary period in history, there can be no denial—despite some misguided people's efforts to the contrary. Certainly, never before had an entire nation organized its power and mobilized itself so efficiently for the sole purpose of destroying human life. Yet the Holocaust was not unique in terms of the number of people murdered; nor was it unique in the brutality of the hatred on which it fed.

A subject such as this raises many questions. How could the Holocaust have happened? Could it have been prevented? How can we keep this from happening again? We have done our best to explore the questions we feel are most central. Ultimately, however, the most compelling questions to emerge from learning about the Holocaust are for each individual reader to answer.

Forever Outsiders

JEWS AND HISTORY FROM ANCIENT TIMES TO AUGUST 1935

By
Linda Jacobs Altman

Academic Editor:
Dr. William L. Shulman
President, Association of Holocaust Organizations
Director, Holocaust Resource Center & Archives, New York

Series Advisor:
Dr. Michael Berenbaum
President & CEO of Survivors of the
Shoah Visual History Foundation, Los Angeles

Series Editor:
Lisa Clyde Nielsen

Advisory Board:
Dr. Minton Goldman, Associate Professor of Political Science,
Northeastern University, Boston

Kathryn Schindler, Teacher, Laguna Niguel Middle School, California;
multicultural and tolerance educator

Kathryn Greenberg, Educational and public-administration specialist,
Chicago Department of Public Health, Division of School Health

Rachel Kubersky, BA Library Education, MPH

Joachim Kalter, Holocaust survivor

A   B L A C K B I R C H   P R E S S   B O O K

W O O D B R I D G E ,   C O N N E C T I C U T

Acknowledgments

Many people have given generously of their time and knowledge during the development of this series. We would like to thank the following people in particular: Genya Markon, and the staff at the United States Holocaust Memorial Museum Photo Archives—Leslie Swift, Sharon Muller, Alex Rossino, and Teresa Pollin—for their talented guidance; and Dr. Michael Berenbaum, currently President and CEO of the Survivors of the Shoah Visual History Foundation and formerly Director of the Research Institute at the U.S. Holocaust Memorial Museum for his valuable editorial input and enthusiastic support of our efforts.

Dr. William L. Shulman, President of the Association of Holocaust Organizations and Director of the Holocaust Resource Center & Archives at Queensborough Community College, merits special mention. As the series academic editor—as well as the compiler of Books 7 and 8—Dr. Shulman's guidance, insight, and dedication went far beyond the call of duty. His deep and thorough knowledge of the subject gave us all the critical perspective we needed to make this series a reality.

Published by Blackbirch Press, Inc.
260 Amity Road
Woodbridge, CT 06525

web site: http://www.blackbirch.com
e-mail: staff@blackbirch.com

©1998 Blackbirch Press, Inc.
First Edition

Printed in the United States of America

10 9 8 7 6 5 4 3 2 1

Cover: A detail from the Arch of Titus in Rome, Italy, that shows the Romans carrying off the spoils of Jerusalem after 70 c.e. (Scala/Art Resource, NY).

Library of Congress Cataloging-in-Publication Data

Altman, Linda Jacobs, 1943–
    Forever outsiders: Jews and history from ancient times to August 1935/ by Linda Jacobs Altman.
        p.   cm. — (Holocaust)
    Includes bibliographical references and index.
    ISBN 1-56711-200-5 (library binding: alk. paper)
    I. Title. II. Series: Holocaust (Woodbridge, Conn.)
DS145.A538   1998
940.53'18—dc21

             96-48179
             CIP
             AC

Foreword

There is a paradox in the study of the Holocaust: The more distant we are from the Event, the more interest seems to grow. In the immediate aftermath of the Holocaust, horrific images were played in movie theaters on newsreels, which was how people saw the news in an era before television. Broadcasting on CBS radio, famed newscaster Edward R. Murrow said:

Permit me to tell you what you would have seen and heard had you been with me on Thursday. It will not be pleasant listening. If you are at lunch or have no appetite to hear of what Germans have done, now is a good time to turn off your radio, for I propose to tell you of Buchenwald.

Murrow described the sights and sounds of what he had experienced in the immediate aftermath of liberation, and his audience was appropriately horrified. Action was required, trials were soon held—an accounting for a deed that was beyond human comprehension, a crime beyond a name, that we now call the "Holocaust."

Shortly thereafter, interest waned. Other topics of the era took center stage—the Cold War, the Berlin blockade, the Korean War—and it seemed for a time that the Holocaust would be forgotten. In retrospect, we can surmise that the silence was a necessary response to such catastrophe. Distance was needed before we could look back and muster enough courage to confront an event so terrible.

No one could have imagined that, half a century after the Holocaust, museums such as the United States Holocaust Memorial Museum would be built and would attract millions of visitors each year. No one, too, would have guessed that films such as *Schindler's List* would be seen by tens of millions of people throughout the world. No one could have foreseen that thousands of books would be published on the subject and courses in schools all over the world would be taught—that interest in this horrible chapter of history would intensify rather than recede with the passage of time.

Why study the Holocaust?

The answer is simple: Because it happened!

An event of such magnitude, a state-sponsored annihilation of an entire people—men, women, and children—must be confronted. Some people have portrayed the Holocaust as an aberration, a world apart from the ordinary world in which we dwell. Even the most eloquent of survivors, Elie Wiesel, calls it the "Kingdom of Night." Yet, to me the Holocaust is not an aberration, but an expression in the extreme of a common thread that runs through our civilization. And thus, not to confront the Event is not to probe the deep darkness that is possible within our world.

Because it happened, we must seek to understand the anguish of the victims—the men, women, and children who faced death and had impossible choices to make, and who could do so little to determine their fate. And we must seek to understand the neutrality and indifference of the bystanders around the world; and what caused the Allies—who were fighting a full-scale world war against the Germans and other Axis powers—to fail to address the "second war," the war against the Jews.

We must also seek to understand the all-too-few non-Jewish heroes of the Holocaust—the men, women, and children who opened their homes and their hearts and provided a haven for the victims; a place to sleep, a crust of bread, a kind word, a hiding place. What makes such goodness possible? Why were they immune to the infection of evil?

We must understand that the Holocaust did not begin with mass killing. Age-old prejudice led to discrimination, discrimination led to persecution, persecution to incarceration, incarceration to annihilation. And mass murder, which culminated with the killing of approximately 6 million Jews, did not begin with the Jews—nor did it encompass only the Jews. The state-sponsored murder of the physically and mentally disabled was a precursor to the Holocaust. It was in that killing process that gas chambers and crematoria were developed and refined, and the staff of the death camps were trained. Romani (commonly but incorrectly referred to as Gypsies) were killed alongside the Jews. Jehovah's Witnesses, German and Austrian male homosexuals, political prisoners and dissidents were also incarcerated in concentration camps, where many were murdered. Gentile and Jewish Poles were subjected to decimation and destruction of their national identity. Though many Jews suffered alone, abandoned and forgotten by the world, they were not the only ones to die.

The study of the Holocaust is not easy. We are often unclear about whose history is being taught: German history, Jewish history, American history, European history. And to understand it, we need to understand more than history. Other disciplines are essential, such as psychology and sociology, political science, philosophy and theology, and, most especially, ethics. When we study the Holocaust, we are forced to face evil, to confront experiences that are horrific and destructive. And even despite the tools of all these disciplines, we still may not understand. Comprehension may elude us.

With the renewed interest in the Holocaust—especially in North America—we have seen that the study of all these deaths is actually in the service of life; the study of evil actually strengthens decency and goodness. For us as free citizens, confronting this European event brings us a new recognition of the principles of constitutional democracy: a belief in equality and equal justice under law; a commitment to pluralism and toleration; a determination to restrain government by checks and balances and by the constitutional protection of "inalienable rights"; and a struggle for human rights as a core value.

The Holocaust shatters the myth of innocence and, at the same time, has implications for the exercise of power. Those who wrestle with its darkness know it can happen again—even in the most advanced, most cultured, most "civilized" of societies. But, if we are faithful to the best of human values, the most sterling of our traditions, then we can have confidence that it "won't happen here." These truths are not self-evident; they are precarious and, therefore, even more precious.

The Holocaust has implications for us as individuals. As we read these books, we can't help but ask ourselves, "What would I have done?" "If I were a Jew, would I have had the courage to resist—spiritually or militarily—and when?" "Would I have had the wisdom and the ability to flee to a place that offered a haven?" "Do I have a friend who would offer me a place of shelter, a piece of bread, a moment of refuge?" "What could I have done to protect my family, to preserve my life?"

We can't offer easy answers because the options were few, the pressures extreme, the conditions unbearable, and the stakes ultimate—life or death.

We may also ask ourselves even more difficult questions: "What prejudices do I have?" "Do I treat all people with full human dignity?" "Am I willing to discriminate against some, to scapegoat others?" "Am I certain—truly certain—that I could not be a killer? That I would not submit to the pressures of conformity and participate in horrible deeds or, worse yet, embrace a belief that makes me certain—absolutely certain—that I am right and the others are wrong? That my cause is just and the other is an enemy who threatens me, who must be eliminated?" These are questions you will ask as you read these books—ask, but not answer.

Perhaps, in truth, the more intensely you read these books, the less certainty you will have in offering your personal answer. Premature answers are often immature answers. Good questions invite one to struggle with basic values.

The central theme of the story of the Holocaust is not regeneration and rebirth, goodness or resistance, liberation or justice, but, rather, death and destruction, dehumanization and devastation, and above all, loss.

The killers were "civilized" men and women of an advanced culture. They were both ordinary and extraordinary, a true cross-section of the men and women of Germany, its allies, and their collaborators, as well as the best and the brightest. In these volumes, those deeds will be seen, as will the evolution of policy, the expansion of the power of the state, and technological and scientific murders unchecked by moral, social, religious, or political constraints. Whether restricted to the past or a harbinger of the future, the killers demonstrated that systematic mass destruction is possible. Under contemporary conditions, the execution of such a policy would only be easier.

The Holocaust transforms our understanding. It shatters faith—religious faith in God and secular faith in human goodness. Its truth has been told not to provide answers, but to raise questions. To live conscientiously in its aftermath, one must confront the reality of radical evil and its past triumphs. At the same time, we must fight against that evil and its potential triumphs in the future.

The call from the victims—from the world of the dead—is to remember. From the survivors, initial silence has given way to testimony. The burden of memory has been transmitted and thus shared. From scholars, philosophers, poets, and artists—those who were there and those who were not—we hear the urgency of memory, its agony and anguish, its meaning and the absence of meaning. To live in our age, one must face the void.

Israel Ba'al Shem Tov, the founder of Hasidism, once said:

*In forgetfulness is the root of exile.
In remembrance, the seed of
redemption.*

His fears of forgetting, we understand all too well.

Whether we can share his hope of remembrance is uncertain.

Still, it is up to us to create that hope.

**Michael Berenbaum
Survivors of the Shoah
Visual History Foundation
Los Angeles, California**

"No One Left to Speak for Me"

In April and May 1945, World War II finally ground to a close in Europe. During that time, the Allied troops who liberated thousands of prisoners in Nazi death and labor camps encountered horrors beyond their wildest imaginations: gas chambers disguised as shower rooms; huge ovens for burning bodies; tomblike barracks where thousands of hollow-eyed prisoners lay dying from starvation, exposure, disease, and beatings.

Stunned and shaken, the liberators were witnessing evidence of a hatred that had run so deep, and for so long, that it had resulted in genocide—the planned murder of an entire people. Under Adolf Hitler, the dictator of Germany from 1933 to 1945,

A Jewish man is forced to cut off the beard of another Jew in Poland, while German officers and local townspeople stand by, watching.

the Nazi Party and its collaborators systematically murdered approximately 6 million Jews in Europe. In their zeal to rid Germany of what they considered lesser beings, the Nazis killed perhaps as many as 4 million other people. The lives of countless others were shattered.

Just Standing By

Thousands, perhaps millions, of ordinary people—businesspeople, neighbors, clergy, schoolmates—played a critical part in making mass murder happen. It was not just the Nazis, not just the wardens of the camps, who made this genocide possible.

Nor was it just Germans. The Nazis' virulent crusade against the Jews and other groups was reported around the world. Yet even the most powerful world leaders of the time failed to put an end to Hitler's brand of terrorism.

By not speaking up against the Nazi regime . . . by not intervening as persecution mounted . . . by just standing by—in all of these ways, and more, ordinary people participated in the Nazis' deadly aim.

German clergyman Martin Niemöller explained the dynamics of participation, passivity, and collaboration during that period, one of the darkest chapters in human history, which came to be termed the Holocaust:

German citizens from Ludgwigslust walk through a concentration camp building in May 1945. Local townspeople were ordered to witness these conditions by American liberating forces.

> First they came for the socialists, and I did not speak out—because I was not a socialist. Then they came for the trade-unionists, and I did not speak out—because I was not a trade-unionist. Then they came for the Jews, and I did not speak out— because I was not a Jew. Then they came for me—and there was no one left to speak for me.

Forever Outsiders

Fanning the Flames of Hatred

A major factor that contributed to this passivity was anti-semitism—hatred of Jews (who are sometimes called "Semites"). The word *antisemitism* didn't exist until 1879, when a German writer named Wilhelm Marr coined it to describe his own deep and abiding hatred. The prejudice against Jewish people that the word describes, however, has existed for centuries.

Expressions of antisemitism over time have swelled and subsided, like ocean waves, in different eras and places around the world. In many societies, Jews have been treated as equals with other respectable citizens. And not all Gentiles (non-Jews) have been antisemitic.

Yet it is also true that, among many peoples, fear and hatred of Jews has shown itself again and again. It has persisted since the dawn of Christianity. The disturbing view of Jews as somehow fundamentally "different," as eternal "outsiders"—endures.

Over the years, many scholars have studied antisemitism in an attempt to understand it. To this end, and perhaps in the hope of ending the phenomenon, some have tried to explain how antisemitism arises and expresses itself.

One approach was put forward by historian Leon Poliakov. He suggested that, through the ages, there have been three main expressions of antisemitism: social and political, religious, and racial. He observed that the forms overlap one another and that different types have dominated at different periods of history.

Other scholars cite stereotypes as the key factors in the development of antisemitism. Not only do they spring from antisemitism, but they also give rise to it. Among the stereotypes that have emerged over the centuries are ugly portrayals of Jews as economic exploiters, as carriers of disease, even as servants of the Devil and killers of Christian children.

Historian Bernard Lazare argued that true antisemitism does not begin until Jews "settle as immigrants in foreign countries and come into contact with natives or older settlers, whose customs, race and religion are different." This explanation touches on the

The Jewish–Christian Split

Christians often ask why Jews did not accept Jesus as the Christ, the Messiah. After all, Jesus lived and died a practicing Jew. Much of his teaching is rooted in Judaism; and to some Jews, Jesus is an important teacher. But to all Jews, Jesus is neither the Messiah nor a God. For according to Jewish teaching, the Messiah is to bring the end of history and the redemption of humanity. Thus, Jews continue to pray for the Messiah, even as they believe that the world is not redeemed.

No discussion of antisemitism is complete without confronting the painful and divisive accusation by some Christians that the Jews killed Jesus (though much of Christian teaching no longer holds modern-day Jews responsible for the execution). It is commonly accepted by biblical scholars and historians alike that crucifixion (the form of execution used to murder Jesus) was a Roman form of punishment. Such power was in the hands of Romans, not Jews. Jews of the first century did not have the power to execute prisoners or to carry out capital punishment—even if they had wanted to.

There was also a long-held view in some Christian teachings that Christianity had come to replace Judaism, the New Testament to replace the "Old," and that Christians were the "true Israel" of the spirit and not of just the flesh. This tradition, known as the supercessionist view, left no room for the continued existence of Jews as a people of God, no place for a continuing Jewish covenant with God. It was a small leap from the idea that the Jews had no reason to continue as a religious community to the idea that Jews had no right to exist.

After the Holocaust, many Christian churches, including the Roman Catholic Church and the Lutheran Church, qualified their teachings so future believers would understand that authentic Christianity does not have to deny the covenant between Jews and God. Judaism and Christianity can co-exist. Jews and Christians can live together, with mutual respect for each other as individuals and also as religious communities.

tendency of human beings to fear and mistrust people who are different from themselves—who are "outside" the larger population. Over time, some members of the majority group develop negative beliefs about the "outsiders" to relieve their own discomfort.

The tide of antisemitism had swept in at various points in Germany's long and complex history. But never had it been as shocking and radical as during the Nazi era: Hitler, manic and charismatic, was able to fan the flames of an ancient hatred into a conflagration.

Transforming Religion into Race

Judaism is a religion. Jews themselves define as "Jewish" anyone who has a Jewish mother (unless the person has converted to another faith) and anyone who has converted to Judaism.

Hitler and the Nazis did not persecute Jews for practicing their religion. Rather, they did so because they believed that Jews were an inferior "race." Jews were impure, they said—and "polluting of German blood." Wrote Hitler in 1924: ". . . a racially pure people which is conscious of its blood can never be enslaved by the Jew." In a book published in 1928, he elaborated upon his bizarre and paranoid beliefs about Jewish people:

> *Jewry . . . has special intrinsic characteristics which separate it from all other peoples living on the globe. Jewry is not a religious community . . . [it] is in reality the . . . governmental system of the Jewish people. . . . The Jewish people cannot carry out the construction of a state . . . hence the ultimate goal of the Jewish struggle for existence is the enslavement of productively active peoples.*

The conception of Jewishness as a "race" was entirely wrong—a religion, whether Judaism or Catholicism or Islam, is a set of beliefs and prescribed customs for expressing and practicing those beliefs. But the Nazis' argument would have dire consequences for Jews in the 1930s and '40s. The Nazis would use it as a "rationale" for an attempt to exterminate European Jewry, a plan known as the "Final Solution of the Jewish Problem" (or Jewish Question).

"The War Against the Jews"

Historian Michael Berenbaum commented that Lucy Dawidowicz, another eminent scholar, called the Holocaust "The War Against the Jews." World War II was not just about Hitler's lust for political power. It was also about his singular drive for the extermination of a people. Learning something of the history of the Jews, therefore, is central to an understanding of the Holocaust.

The "Chosen People"

The Holocaust was a pivotal event in the history of the Jews, and its significance should never be understated. But Jewish history neither begins nor ends with that tragic period and the virulent antisemitism that led to it. It is the story of the development and evolution of probably the oldest surviving religion in the world and the vibrantly diverse people who ascribe to it. It is also the story of that people's survival, through good times and bad.

A Singular God

The religion known as Judaism began with Abraham, who is believed to have lived around the time 1800 to 1600 B.C.E. in Mesopotamia, a region of what, today, is often referred to as the "Middle East." In an era when others worshipped idols and natural

----

Abraham, who worshipped a singular God, is known as the "father of Judaism." Here, he is shown with his son Isaac.

* B.C.E.= Before the Common Era; C.E.= Common Era

forces such as wind and fire, Abraham worshipped one all-powerful Creator—a singular God—who was without form or substance. This, wrote historian Robert Seltzer, "was not 'a god,' but God, a being whose nature is unique, absolute, and ultimate."

Abraham's radical new religious idea is known today as monotheism, the worship of one God. Abraham and his descendants—the "chosen people"—were called upon to serve God. One day, they would receive and protect God's own Torah (sacred text).

During the following centuries, Judaism grew into a complex system of legal and moral guidelines. Eventually, the religion provided Jews with laws, customs, and rules that shaped every part of their lives.

Historian Bernard Lazare explained it this way:

> Not only did [God] say to the Jews, "Ye shall believe in the one God and ye shall worship no idols," he also prescribed for them rules of hygiene and morality. . . . Each of the given laws, whether agrarian, civil, prophylactic [health-preserving], theological, or moral, proceeded from the same authority, so that all these codes formed a whole.

The early Hebrews (as the Jews were originally known) were few in number and led simple lives. Over the centuries, however, the Jewish population grew and became more diverse, from merchants in Jerusalem to nomadic herders in the desert. In turn, the beliefs and practices of Judaism also became more complex. The religion revealed one of the characteristics that define it to this day—diversity and adaptation within a strongly held tradition. Other major beliefs that would emerge in Judaism were the concept of treating others as one would wish to be treated, and the idea of God's justice in contrast to the evil and suffering in the world.

A Crossroads of the World

The first Hebrews lived in a part of the world that would come to be called Palestine. Then, as now, it was at a vital crossroads, situated between the vast continents of Asia, Africa, and Europe.

Palestine and the surrounding region lay on a lucrative trade route, whether for spices or other commodities—or for ideas. The land itself, a complex of distinct geographical zones, was also desirable. Much of the landscape was harsh and forbidding. But with proper planning and management—the building of irrigation canals, dutiful tending of farm plots, careful stewardship of herds—the Jews and other groups in the region were often able not only to survive but also to prosper. It was a region where the industrious could make a home, or a homeland.

The Spread of Empires

The promise of the region of Palestine had long been noted. Since the earliest civilizations in the Middle East, various political leaders had competed for power over this central land and its peoples. In the two millennia after the time of Abraham, some of the world's great empires too would seek to wrest control. These struggles would at times cause a dispersion—called a diaspora—of the Jews. Seeking peace and freedom, many would settle in other regions.

During these centuries, people were struggling not only for political control; they also wanted their spiritual beliefs to be accepted. A number of different belief systems existed, and over the course of time, people's different beliefs would not only influence but enrich one another.

The vast Persian Empire held sway in the region beginning in the 500s B.C.E., followed by the Greeks, led by Alexander the Great, in the 300s B.C.E. Yet, even as the Greek Empire began to fall to the Romans, Judaism was still the only monotheistic religion. Wrote historian Robert Seltzer:

> *The Jews and their Scriptures were beginning to impinge on the pagan world to a degree that had not been possible previously. Armed with the idea of bearing witness to the one God and the expectation that paganism was finished, a highly unusual people and their religion were not going to be ignored, nor were they going to let themselves be ignored.*

Roman Domination

The Jews vigorously resisted foreign occupation. Not even the expansionist forces of the mighty Roman Republic (509 B.C.E. to 27 B.C.E.) and Roman Empire (27 B.C.E. to circa 480 C.E.) could bring the Jews under their control.

In 66 C.E., the Jews rebelled fiercely against Roman conquest, but it was a hopeless battle—the Romans' military machine was so strong that no one could stop them. This bitter conflict ended with the destruction of the Jews' sacred Temple at Jerusalem in 70 C.E. This temple had been at the center of Jewish life and faith for generations.

Defeat with Daring

Two other rebellions followed, in the years 116 and 132–135 C.E. After the second uprising, the Romans were determined to crush Jewish resistance once and for all. Jews were barred from their Holy City of Jerusalem and were forbidden to practice their religion—on pain of death.

Some Jews managed to stay in Palestine, but many others migrated west and north, to other lands in the Roman Empire. Some moved east, to the lands under the control of the Persians. This was a diaspora—an event that would occur time and again in the history of the Jews, even up to modern times.

The destruction of the Temple in Jerusalem, 70 C.E.

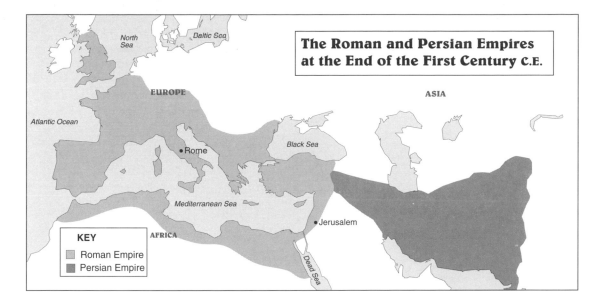

The Roman and Persian Empires at the End of the First Century C.E.

KEY
Roman Empire
Persian Empire

Making a Place

Wherever they settled in the Middle East, Africa, Europe, and Asia (and eventually the Western Hemisphere), diasporic Jews set about making a place for themselves. They worked the land or made a living as artisans, traders, or merchants—sometimes alongside non-Jews, and sometimes apart. Everywhere they established vibrant communities, some of which have endured to this day. Observed Robert Seltzer:

> A remark attributed to the Greek geographer Strabo, partly true in his time [the first century B.C.E], was certainly characteristic of the Roman empire at its height: "This people [the Jews] has already made its way into every city, and it is not easy to find any place in the habitable world which has not received this nation and in which it has not made its power felt."

These early centuries of the Common Era were a time of intense religious diversity and feeling, leading in some places to great cultural exchanges and challenges. The prosperous and sophisticated Sassanian Babylonia (Iran), a part of the Persian Empire, was one such place. There, many diverse religions and forms of thought flourished. Jewish thought, too, thrived in this stimulating environment.

"Do You Wish to Convert?"

The rise and fall of the Roman Empire was a time of upheaval for many peoples. Christianity took firm hold in the centuries after the fall of the empire, causing great changes in how people in many lands thought and lived.

Jews were also changing during this period. They settled farther into Europe, Africa, and Asia. And more and more they became an urban people, often earning their livelihood in trade and crafts rather than by the soil. Though many Jews were very poor, others prospered. But everywhere they developed a rich variety of cultural and religious traditions.

They were scattered throughout many lands, but the different Jewish communities kept close ties. Thus, while they were a minority in every country, they were a cohesive people.

Torture wheels such as this were used during the Spanish Inquisition to try to get converted Jews and Muslims to "confess" that they were again following their old religions.

A Foundation of Hatred

During the early centuries of Christianity, which began with Jesus some 2,000 years ago, antisemitism became woven into the religion's very fabric of belief. Eventually, the official position of the Roman Catholic Church would be that the Jews had killed Jesus—to Christians, the Messiah and Son of God.

In fact, however, it was actually Roman soldiers, acting under Roman law, who had executed Jesus, claiming that he was a revolutionary leader. But Christians still believed that the Jews were responsible. (It would not be until 1965 that the Roman Catholic Church officially declared that contemporary Jews should not be held responsible for the murder of Jesus.)

Conflicts of Belief

Several core beliefs of Christianity were completely incompatible with the foundations of Judaism. The Jews believed in their one true God, which meant that they could not accept a Christian God—one who existed in three parts, or "persons" (the Father, the Son, and the Holy Ghost). The Jews also believed that there should be no physical representation of God. Thus, they could not believe in a Christian God who took human form—or any physical form, for that matter.

The Christian claim that faith in Jesus should replace observance of the law also went against Jewish belief. To Jews, the law as given to them in the Torah was more than a set of regulations to be obeyed—it was a living and holy thing, a way of life established for them directly by God. To Christians, however, Judaism was a "lesser" truth sent by God to prepare the way for the "greater" truth of Christianity.

Jews in Medieval Europe

Despite their differences in religious beliefs, Jews and Christians often lived peaceably in medieval Europe (roughly 500 to 1500 C.E., often called the Middle Ages). In many communities, the two groups co-existed in matters of worship and livelihood.

The Ashkenazic and Sephardic Jews in Europe

The Jews who followed the spread of Islam into Spain and Africa beginning in the mid-600s C.E. went as pioneers, not as prisoners or refugees. Mostly educated urban-dwellers, they developed a rich religious tradition based on the Babylonian Talmud. They became known as Sephardic Jews.

Another group of dispersed Jews, who would become known as the Ashkenazim, moved into Central and Eastern Europe. Many were very poor, living in small villages called *shtetls*. But, despite harsh conditions, they developed a vivid folk culture that nurtured and sustained them. Jewish learning and Jewish piety were the pillars of that culture, and they proved to be amazingly strong, even in the face of persecution and hatred.

In some areas, however, Jews were forced to live as "outsiders" on the fringes of community life. Many countries did not allow Jews to own land, to testify in court against a Christian, even to enter certain trades and professions.

Under these circumstances, many Jews eked out a living in small trades, such as selling used clothing. Some found a niche for themselves as moneylenders. In this role, Jews were not only tolerated—but desired. The Catholic Church would not allow Christians to lend money at interest; in fact, the Church considered it a sin. This necessary service, then, was left to the Jews.

Huge Risks

In many European towns and villages, peasants borrowed money from Jews to tide them over between harvests. The wealthy did business with Jewish moneylenders to improve their estates—even to finance their wars.

In many regions, the Jews' place in society was not protected by law, because they were not considered full citizens. Thus, Jewish moneylenders often took huge risks; sometimes they were in danger of losing their money altogether. A borrower, for example, might "cancel" his debt to a moneylender by rousing public anger against the Jews. Local political leaders would sometimes gain favor with their subjects by canceling all debts owed to Jews.

The Crusades

On November 27, 1095, Pope Urban II, leader of the Roman Catholic Church, spoke at a great assembly in the town of Clermont, France. He called for a great "Crusade," a religious campaign, against the "infidels" (non-Christians; in this case, Muslims) who now controlled Jerusalem. This was to be the first of eight Crusades, stretching from the 1000s to the 1200s. The Crusaders would be "God's own army," Urban said, restoring the Holy City of Jerusalem to Christian control. To those who joined that army, he promised the remission of sins and life everlasting.

Around the same time, a separate "people's crusade" rallied behind a man known as Peter the Hermit. Peter's followers were mostly poor, uneducated peasants who had their own idea of how to do "God's work." Pope Urban's knights-in-armor wanted to liberate Jerusalem, but Peter's ragtag army just wanted to slaughter infidels—and they saw no reason to wait until they got to Palestine to do it. During the spring of 1096, they swept through the Rhineland (in modern times, part of Germany), attacking Jews wherever they found them—and sometimes murdering them. In the name of Jesus Christ, they destroyed entire Jewish communities in the cities of Worms, Mainz, and Cologne.

Those Jews who were willing to convert to Christianity were generally welcomed by the Crusaders with sincere enthusiasm. But, to the dismay of these "defenders of the faith," as the Crusaders thought of themselves, hundreds of Jews chose *kiddush ha-Shem* (a Hebrew term meaning "martyrdom") rather than renounce their faith.

One of the chronicles of the era told of a young Jewish man named Isaac ben Daniel. When the Crusaders asked him to deny his religion and accept theirs, he refused. With quiet dignity, he commended his soul to the one God he trusted:

*They put a rope around his neck and dragged him . . . throughout
the city, through the mud of the streets, up to the [church]. . . .
They said to him: "You may still be saved. Do you wish to convert?" He signaled [no] with his finger—for he was unable to utter
a word with his mouth. . . . They severed his neck.*

Like anyone in a desperate situation, the Jews involved in the
Rhineland tragedy reacted in many different ways. Some, like
Isaac ben Daniel, suffered a martyr's death rather than give up

**This woodcut from the late 1400s depicts the Jews of Cologne being burned alive in 1096, during
the Crusades.**

their religion. Others were killed resisting; some took their own lives. And some accepted Christian baptism to save themselves and their families.

Dark Visions of "Evil"

On occasion, great public anger toward the Jews was incited by accusing them of hideous crimes. As the Middle Ages wore on in Europe, widespread notions about the "nature" of Jews became profoundly disturbing. Many people began to suspect that Jews were inherently evil and that they posed a danger to the "good Christians" of the world. Wrote historian Norman Cohn:

> *From the time of the first crusade onwards Jews were presented as children of the Devil, agents employed by Satan for the expressed purpose of combatting Christianity and harming Christians. . . . Above all it was said that Jews worshipped the Devil, who rewarded them collectively by making them masters of black magic; so that however helpless individual Jews might seem, Jewry possessed limitless powers for evil.*

This dark and insidious vision of the Jewish "evil" gave rise to the extremely inflammatory idea that Jews used the blood of Christian children in their religious rites. This suspicion led to a rabid, often deadly form of persecution known as "blood libel"— a charge of ritual murder. It was entirely false, but many people believed it.

The first recorded case of blood libel occurred in Norwich, England, during the spring of 1144. The Jews were preparing for Passover—an important holiday that marks their ancestors' legendary escape from slavery in Egypt (the Exodus)—when a Christian boy named William disappeared from his home. Some of the Christian townspeople connected the boy's disappearance to the religious preparations that were being made. From there, rumors spread that the boy had been kidnapped for use in a ritual Passover sacrifice.

This woodcut from the fifteenth century depicts a commonly believed "blood libel" scene, where "Jews" supposedly surround a Christian boy for ritual murder.

William was eventually found dead, but his body showed no evidence of foul play. No one was charged with murder. However, the sinister rumors and suspicions that continued to swirl about the Jews had already taken their toll.

The blood-libel curse spread across Europe like an epidemic. In 1171, all the Jews in Blois, France, were burned alive after being accused of ritual murder. In 1255, a particularly cruel blood libel sent 19 Jews to the gallows. Chronicler Matthew Paris "recorded" the tale in language guaranteed to rouse Christian fury:

> . . . the Jews . . . stole a child called Hugh, being eight years old . . . [and] by the consent of all, the child [was] . . . whipped even unto blood . . . crowned with thorns, wearied with spitting and strikings . . . and after [all this], they crucified him.

As the idea of blood libel became more and more entrenched in Christian beliefs, it gave rise to other, similar accusations. These charges—as entirely unfounded as blood libel—were nonetheless deeply offensive and disturbing to Christians.

The accusation of "Host desecration" was one of the most widely believed charges. The Church taught that the wafer, or Host, of Holy Communion became the true body of Jesus Christ. To damage the Host was, in effect, to crucify Jesus all over again. It was said that Jews held unspeakable ceremonies in which they "tortured" stolen wafers with knives and needles. According to popular legend, the Host shed blood with every wound.

Starting Over

Blood libel and Host desecration were perhaps the two most powerful accusations that roused hatred toward Jews. But they were part of a larger fear and resentment that grew during the Middle Ages. When popular hatred rose to a fever pitch, some governments "solved the problem" by getting rid of the Jews. England expelled them in 1290; France did so a century later.

Some of these Jews moved into Germany; later groups migrated farther east, to Poland and Russia. Once again, the Jews set about rebuilding their lives—and once again, they proved their ability to survive, and often even to prosper. Indeed, despite occasional periods of persecution, Jewish communities became well established in Central and Eastern Europe. Great centers of learning and commerce sprang up.

Some Important Centers of
Jewish Population in Europe,
1000s–1400s C.E.

The "Black Death"

In 1347, bubonic plague—a highly infectious disease—struck
Europe. With only crude forms of medicine to combat the
plague, people died by the tens of thousands. The disease
spread throughout Europe at lightning speed. By the time it
subsided, an estimated 25 million people had died. In fact,
so many people died so fast that, often, there wasn't time for
proper funerals, or even grief.

In many towns across Europe, carts lumbered through cobble-stone streets. The crier tolled his bell and spoke his macabre request: "Bring out your dead, bring out your dead." The carts quickly filled with corpses.

Nobody knew what caused the "Black Death." Some said it was God's punishment for the sins of humankind. Others said it was brought by the Jews. From hatred of all things Christian and their powers of "black magic," they argued, the Jews had poisoned the wells from which people drew their drinking water.

In many parts of Europe, Jews were falsely blamed for causing the "Black Death," which killed an estimated 25 million people in the mid- and late 1300s.

To many desperate and dying people, this scenario seemed believable. Since there was no other clear explanation for the terrible pain and suffering they saw, blaming the Jews offered a convenient answer.

During the first Crusade, the Christians of Mainz had killed approximately 1,000 Jews for refusing to accept Christianity. During the Black Death, they killed some 6,000 Jews for "poisoning the wells." The people of Strasbourg herded 2,000 Jewish men, women, and children onto a wooden platform built over a deep pit. While the Christians watched and prayed, the Jews were burned alive, their bodies falling into a waiting grave.

The Spanish Inquisition

In 1480, religious leaders in Spain embarked on a "crusade" of their own. This one, known as the Spanish Inquisition, was not aimed at practicing Jews but at heretics (Christians who held forbidden doctrines, called heresies) and *conversos* (former Jews who had accepted Christianity).

"Grand Inquisitor" Tómas de Torquemada began his ruthless program with a search for "secret Jews"—people who had been forced to convert publicly to Christianity but who still practiced Judaism in private. Those he found were tortured until they "confessed" their heresies.

In time, Torquemada went beyond seeking out Jews who were only pretending to be Christians. He began to look for signs of "Jewish" belief or behavior in the *conversos*. His followers found hundreds who still "behaved in a festive manner" on Jewish holidays or who enjoyed Jewish food.

The "Grand Inquisitor" finally decided that no Jews could be trusted. The only way to root out "Jewish tendencies," he believed, was to expel all unconverted Jews from Spain. In March 1492, Spain's King Ferdinand and Queen Isabella signed an "edict of expulsion," giving the Jews four months to convert to Christianity—or leave. Many did leave, some choosing to migrate to the Ottoman (Turkish) Empire to the east.

The Reformation

Soon after the Spanish Jews were exiled by the Catholic Church, German Jews faced new threats from the Protestant Reformation. This religious movement began in 1517, when a German monk named Martin Luther challenged the power of the Catholic Church. He didn't believe that the Roman Catholic pope was infallible or that obedience to Church teachings guaranteed everlasting life. Salvation came by faith in Christ, he said; the Church could neither grant it nor withhold it.

In his early writings, Luther was friendly toward the Jews. He thought that certain "errors" in the doctrines of the Catholic Church were all that kept Jews from embracing Christianity as the one "true faith." He was convinced that, if these "errors" were addressed, the Jews would convert. In an essay written in 1523, Luther argued:

> [The Catholics] have dealt with the Jews as if they were dogs and not human beings. They have done nothing for them but curse them and seize their wealth. I would advise and beg everybody to deal kindly with the Jews and to instruct them in the Scriptures. . . . We must receive them kindly and allow them to compete with us in earning a livelihood . . . and if some remain [stubborn], what of it? Not everyone is a good Christian.

In time, however, Luther realized that altering Church doctrine would not change things: Jews simply did not want to be converted to any other religion. What he perceived as their stubborn nonbelief infuriated him. And with this drastic change came a drastic new stance: Luther now turned wholeheartedly against the Jews, penning some of the harshest antisemitic attacks ever written. In one essay from 1544, Luther wrote:

> Set their synagogues on fire, and whatever does not burn up should be covered or spread over with dirt so that no man may ever be able to see a cinder or a stone of it . . . their homes should likewise be broken down and destroyed. . . . They shall be put

The German monk Martin Luther—the founder of Protestantism—turned against the Jews in the mid-1500s and advocated their total destruction.

under one roof, or in a stable . . . in order that they may realize that they are not masters in our land, as they boast, but miserable captives. . . . They should be deprived of their prayer books and Talmuds in which such idolatry, lies, cursing and blasphemy are taught. . . . Their rabbis must be forbidden to teach under threat of death.

Luther's followers now had a clear mandate to target Jews for destruction. As had sometimes been the case for centuries before, religious zealotry and deep-seated prejudices combined to form a powerful, and ultimately devastating, threat for Europe's Jews. And nearly 400 years later, Martin Luther's writings would be read and considered by a young Austrian political upstart named Adolf Hitler.

Freedom and Fear

Jewish history has been the story of the rise and evolution of rich and diverse community life—occasionally punctuated by incidents of persecution. This is true of Jewish history in the Europe of the early modern era—the 1500s and 1600s.

Even during the worst periods of antisemitism in the Middle Ages, such as the frenzied accusations of blood libel, Jewish life had gone on. Many Jewish communities had arisen and developed throughout Europe. Jewish religious and intellectual life increasingly enriched the continent. Poland, for example, became a center of Jewish scholarship in the 1500s. The Jewish middle class was expanding in most of Europe. With this prosperity came an explosion of intellectual growth, with Jews providing important contributions in philosophy, science, the arts, and literature.

This engraving depicts the expulsion of Jews from the Russian town of Tedolsk in the late 1800s.

------- "Merchant Princes" and International Financiers -------

In about 1590, a group of Marranos, the "secret Jews" of Spain, went to Holland seeking religious freedom. They were the descendants of Spanish Jews who had avoided the expulsion order of 1492 by "converting" to Christianity and continuing to practice Judaism in secret. In the city of Amsterdam, they found the freedom they sought. Other Jews soon followed, many of them wealthy and well educated. Some helped to build new industries, establish new trade routes, and develop international finance into a powerful economic tool. With their help, the seventeenth century became known as the "golden age of the Netherlands."

When Oliver Cromwell became Lord Protector of England in 1653, he wasted no time in moving the British economy toward a free-enterprise system, which encouraged the growth of a strong middle class and placed a new emphasis on international trade. The Jewish financiers and "merchant princes" of Amsterdam now found an opportunity to expand their horizons in England. Jews quickly excelled in commerce and international finance there.

The Jewish community of England produced a number of figures who became prominent in the Gentile world. Sir Moses Montefiore (1784–1885) made a fortune as an investment banker and earned knighthood along the way. He was a champion of human rights who endowed schools, orphanages, and hospitals, and campaigned for Jewish emancipation in England. Two years before that emancipation became official, Lionel de Rothschild—of a well-known German Jewish banking family—became the first Jew to win a seat in the British House of Commons (1858).

Such achievements won both admiration and acceptance for prominent Jews, but they also triggered a backlash. Anti-Semites began to suggest that a "worldwide Jewish conspiracy" was attempting to seize control of commerce and government. These alarmists ignored the fact that Jews were never more than a tiny minority in international finance. But they were a visible minority, and that made them vulnerable, as the infamous antisemitic tract, *The Protocols of the Elders of Zion,* published in 1903, would demonstrate.

In many lands during the 1500s and 1600s, expressions of antisemitism eased from their worst outbreaks in the Middle Ages—perhaps due to the general improvement in European living standards and learning during this period. Jews gradually found their way back to England and France, countries that had once expelled them. Important Jewish centers rose from London to Prague, from Amsterdam to Bordeaux. In many places, Jews were granted more rights and freedoms than ever before.

The era, however, was not free of antisemitism. Some incidents were worrisome and disturbing for the Jews, but not deadly. For example, the first ghetto was established in 1516 for Jews, in Venice, Italy. In this "Jewish quarter," Jews could be segregated from the larger community. The Talmud was burned in Italy in 1553, and the Catholic Church established censorship of Hebrew books in 1554.

Other events were far more ominous. The Inquisition was introduced permanently into Portugal in 1536, for example, and political troubles in Russia and Poland led to widespread massacres of Jews in the mid-1600s.

The early 1700s, however, were relatively free of persecution. Jews in many European communities gained more rights and freedoms. Some of them were allowed to be autonomous—self-governed according to their own laws and customs. In such an environment of tolerance, European Jewry flourished.

To the Pale

Late in the 1700s, Russia annexed parts of Poland and Ukraine and found itself with a large population of Jews. Most of this population was poor, scratching out a living in *shtetls,* small villages. The Russians didn't know what to do with these people who practiced an unfamiliar religion. In 1772, the ruler of Russia, Czarina Catherine, dealt with this "problem" by declaring the newly annexed lands to be a Jewish "Pale of Settlement."

Eventually, Jews from all over Russia were required to move to the Pale, and those who already lived there were forced to stay. No Jew could leave this designated area without special travel documents or residence permits.

In time, the Russians decided that separation wasn't enough; instead, they wanted to transform these "alien" people into "real" Russians. Their new plans began with Jewish children. Jewish

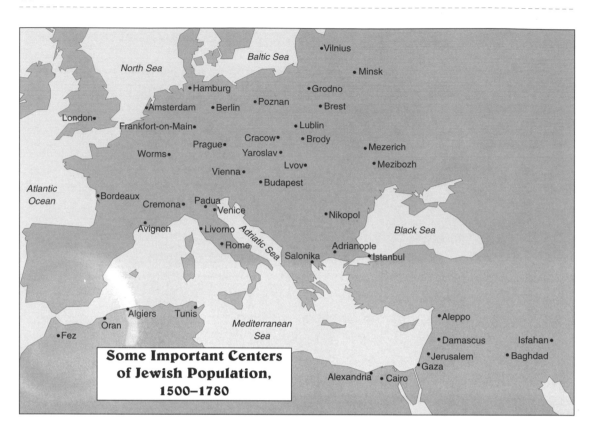

Some Important Centers of Jewish Population, 1500–1780

schools were required to teach all classes in Russian, Polish, or German. The use of Yiddish (the "everyday" dialect spoken in the *shtetls*) and Hebrew was forbidden.

In 1822, Russia began conscripting (forcibly drafting) Jewish 12-year-olds into its army. By decree of the czar, the boys could be forced to serve for 25 years. Few boys who went away to the army ever came home again. Terrified Jewish parents hid their sons, or even maimed them so they would not pass the physical exam.

"In Darkest Russia"

A growing Russian nationalist movement triggered antisemitic violence in the Pale. With the motto "One Russia, one creed, one Czar," nationalists vowed to return their homeland to the source of its greatness: the "Slavic (Russian) soul." The Jews of Russia were to have no part in that soul.

Nationalist leader Konstantin Pobedonostsev actually developed a "formula" for getting rid of Russia's Jews: one-third by conversion, one-third by emigration, one-third by starvation.

Brutal as Pobedonostsev's plan was, the Jews of the Pale did, at least, have two options other than death. Yet most Jews held firm to their religion, a fact that must have angered and confounded the Russians. Without the option of mass conversion, the Russians turned to violence against the Jews. In 1881, militant revolutionaries assassinated Czar Alexander II. Because one member of the group was Jewish, the new czar took revenge on all Jews. He "celebrated" his coronation with a pogrom (an organized mass attack) against Jews in the city of Elizavetgrad.

From there, the terror spread through dozens of towns in the Kiev region, then into other districts. From gangs of peasants with pitchforks to mounted riders with guns, the peasants and

---------------- Yiddish: Language of the Ashkenazi ----------------

Yiddish, the folk language of the Ashkenazi Jews, is rich with imagery that ranges from the sentimental to the sarcastic. Author Leo Rosten explained the origins of Yiddish and its remarkable elasticity in *Hooray for Yiddish!*:

Yiddish uses the letters of the Hebrew, not the Roman, alphabet, and is written or printed from right to left . . . . Hebrew and Yiddish are entirely independent languages. You may be a wizard in Hebrew and not understand a line of Yiddish; the same is true vice versa . . . . [Yiddish] is a "fusion" *language that has drawn upon Hebrew, Loez (Jewish correlates of Latin, Old French, Old Italian), German and Slavic . . . . [Yiddish] favors paradox, because it knows that only paradox can do justice to the injustices of life; it adores irony, because the only way the Jews could retain their sanity was to view a dreadful world with sardonic . . . eyes . . . . Jews had to become psychologists, and their preoccupation with human . . . behavior made Yiddish remarkably rich in names for the [description] of character types . . . .*

An assault on a Jew in Kiev, in the presence of the military.

townspeople came killing, looting, and burning. "In darkest Russia" became a catch-phrase for violence and brutality.

During this period, more than 1 million Jews fled to the United States, France, England, Germany, and other countries. However, many youths stayed in Russia to join Communist revolutionaries who desired a society in which all people—Jews included—would be "comrades" working together for the common good. For a time, these Jews and Gentiles worked together for a common cause. Years later, they fought side by side in the October 1917 revolution that toppled Czar Nicholas II from his throne.

Freedom to the West

In the late 1700s and early 1800s, Jews in Western Europe were enjoying a period of tolerance and enlightenment. From England to France, and from Italy to Denmark and Holland, Jews enjoyed new freedoms. They were now often able to take more active roles in the cultural, economic, and political life of their various countries.

Many German Jews seemed especially eager to join the larger, mainstream society. They adopted the secular (non-religious) customs of the country and even changed some of their religious practices in order to "fit in" more with non-Jewish Germans. They put aside the ancient dietary laws so they could eat and drink with Christian friends. They shaved their beards and spoke German instead of Hebrew or Yiddish.

Despite these changes, however, German antisemitism did not wither away, as the Jews had hoped. Indeed, these deep-seated prejudices soon found expression in new and violent forms.

In the late 1800s, German anti-Semites tried to promote "scientific" explanations for their belief that Jews were an "inferior race," even a dangerous one. And proponents of this "racial science" convinced many German Gentiles that Northern European peoples represented a "master race," genetically superior and more advanced than any other human group.

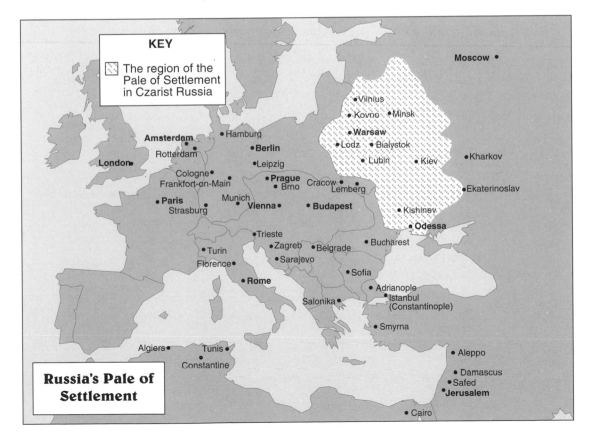

Russia's Pale of Settlement

Shtetls, the small Jewish towns of Eastern Europe and the Russian Pale of Settlement, were often isolated and impoverished, yet these rural communities produced a way of life that was warm, vibrant, and emotionally—if not economically—secure.

The Lithuanian town of Eishishok was such a place. The circumstances of its founding are somewhat unclear. According to a Russian encyclopedia, the town was established in 1070, but it probably did not have a well-established Jewish community until the fourteenth century.

Life in Eishishok revolved around the marketplace, the synagogue, and the home. Jews typically lived in the center of town, their wooden homes clustered around the marketplace. Most people kept a small garden, a few chickens, and perhaps a cow for milk. Tradespeople often maintained stores or workshops in the front of the house.

In her description of Eishishok life, historian Ellen Livingston captured the flavor of a way of life that flourished over the course of centuries:

Until 1930, the sole mode of transportation was horse and wagon . . . .

Electricity arrived in town about the same time, when the Kyutzevsky family funded and built a power station in the market place. . . . Aisheshuk maintained its medieval form as a town of four major streets leading to a central marketplace. . . . The marketplace was the center of communal and economic life, coming alive every Thursday when peasants from the neighboring farms and villages brought their produce to trade with the townspeople. . . . In one corner of town stood the main synagogue. . . . The shul-hoif, the plaza in front of the synagogue, was the site of weddings and other communal celebrations.

This arrangement created a seamless quality to Jewish life—a comfortable union of domestic, social, economic, and religious functions. An Eishishoker (resident of Eishishok) didn't play one

The Dreyfus Affair

One antisemitic scandal of the 1800s did not come out of the chaos of "darkest Russia" but, rather, from freedom-loving France. The press called this scandal the "Dreyfus Affair."

Captain Alfred Dreyfus was the only Jewish officer attached to the General Staff of the French Army, a position that gave him role at home, another at work, and yet another in community or religious activities. Life was all of a piece, and everyone belonged.

The price of that belonging was conformity to principles of Orthodox Judaism, loyalty to one's family, and a willingness to put the good of the community ahead of personal advancement. Nonconformity disrupted the timeless rhythms of this life and was therefore soundly discouraged. As one former resident recalled:

We were children: we didn't want to go to shul [synagogue]. But so people shouldn't say, especially in a small town where everybody knows each other, "You see! His son doesn't go to shul! He goes out in the streets!" —we used to go.

Those who were willing to trade conformity for contentment lived happily in the tight-knit community of Eishishok. Those who wanted to make their own way, however, might eventually leave for a more diversified community.

Jewish women in the small Polish town of Rimanov work together to make lace curtains, circa 1930.

The centuries of Jewish life in Eishishok came to an abrupt end in September 1941, when German killing squads systematically massacred the entire Jewish population in just a few days. Today, a memorial tablet for the "Holy Martyrs of Our City of Aisheshuk (Eishishok)" rests on Mount Zion in Jerusalem, and its people are memorialized in the United States Holocaust Memorial Museum's Hall of Faces, a moving exhibit of 6,000 photographs.

access to highly classified military secrets. In 1894, Dreyfus was accused and convicted of using that access to betray his country.

Anti-Semites pounced on the case. Dreyfus was a Jew, they said, and "everybody knew" that Jews were natural-born traitors. Unless somebody stopped them, they argued, the Jews would take over the nation. Hatreds that had simmered for years now

This antisemitic cartoon, published in an Austrian magazine, read, "In the Dreyfus Affair, the more that is exposed, the more Judah [the Jew] is embarrassed."

came to the surface. In some places, Jews were mocked and attacked in the streets. Few French people participated, but the Dreyfus Affair would have long-lasting effects.

Dreyfus was convicted and sentenced to life imprisonment. After a long and bitter legal struggle, he was cleared of the charges and restored to his army career. But the damage to the Jews of France had already been done. Their hopes for safety, equality, and a life free from antisemitism had been destroyed once again.

Herzl's Call

The Dreyfus case, with its many intrigues, made it painfully obvious that, even if Jews were granted freedom and equality in a modern Europe, these freedoms could not erase the long-standing prejudices against Jews among some Europeans. This realization prompted Austrian journalist Theodor Herzl to action. He had long advocated the creation of a Jewish homeland in Palestine, though he was comfortable in the Gentile world and had believed that antisemitism would gradually disappear as more Jews adapted to that world. Now he believed that this would never happen.

When Albert Dreyfus was stripped of his rank, the angry onlookers didn't shout "Death to traitors" or "Death to Dreyfus." They shouted "Death to Jews." Those words burned into Herzl's consciousness. It was an old story—the story of prejudice: all members of the group (in this case, Jews) being blamed for the real or supposed actions of a single person. Outraged, Herzl wrote:

The Dreyfus case [is] more than a judicial error, it [shows] the desire of . . . the French to condemn a Jew, and to condemn all Jews in this one Jew. "Death to the Jews!" howled the mob, as the [army insignia and badges of rank] were being ripped from the captain's coat. . . . Where? In France. In republican, modern, civilized France, a hundred years after the Declaration of the Rights of Man. The French people . . . [do not] want to extend the rights of man to Jews. The edict of the great [French] Revolution has been revoked.

Herzl was now convinced that Jews could never put an end to antisemitism by behaving more like Gentiles, or even by accepting Christian baptism. At the core of the problem, he reasoned, was the fact that Jews had no homeland to call their own. Thus, no matter how they behaved within the context of a given culture, they would be forever outsiders, and their national loyalties would always be suspect.

To address this problem of "rootlessness," Herzl founded what later came to be called the Zionist movement. The name came from Mount Zion, in Jerusalem, which had long been a symbol of the Jewish "promised land." In 1897, Herzl stood before the First Zionist Congress in Basel, Switzerland. His statement of purpose was clear: "to create for the Jewish people a homeland in Palestine secured by public law."

At the time of his speech, Palestine was a colony of the Ottoman Empire (present-day Turkey). The Turks did not object when Zionists began buying land, paying high prices to anyone who was willing to sell. Once more, the ancestral home beckoned to Jews, and many were eager to answer the call.

In the 1800s, Jewish life in some places was flourishing despite growing antisemitism in other places. In the United States—in New York in particular—many Jews enjoyed prosperity and fair treatment. Here, a New York Jewish family sits down for a Passover seder.

Unsettled Times

The early twentieth century was a time of social and political upheaval, when change happened faster than most people could absorb it. Europe went to war, Russia faced a revolution that replaced its czar with a Communist government, and Zionists continued their struggle to create a homeland in Palestine.

Unsettled times of rapid change had always been dangerous for Jews. As an identifiable minority, they made a ready target for those who were frightened and angered by events they couldn't understand, let alone control. The first two decades of the twentieth century would be no exception to that long-standing tendency.

During World War I, American forces fire on German troops in an advance, 1918.

"Conspiracy" Theories

In 1903, a document of questionable origin entitled *The Protocols of the Elders of Zion* appeared in print for the first time. Along with presenting new stereotypes against Jews, this work incorporated many of the same misconceptions that led to the accusation and conviction of Albert Dreyfus. And it provided a whole new "reason" for hating Jews: The Jews, *The Protocols* stated, were plotting to conquer the world.

The Protocols gained credibility because it was based upon two undisputed truths: Jews considered themselves a single people, and they were scattered throughout all the countries of Europe. Anti-Semites, however, distorted those facts to their own ends.

The Protocols, said the anti-Semites, was a supposed "step-by-step plan" for world conquest and proof that there was, in fact, a Jewish "conspiracy" at work. The roots of the conspiracy idea harkened back hundreds of years, to the Jewish moneylenders of the Middle Ages. During that time, many moneylenders made a comfortable living, but they certainly did not amass great wealth or power.

A few, however, became international bankers at a time when Europe had dozens of currencies and no established rates of exchange. Doing business across national borders was risky and difficult. Some Jews took up the challenge, moving from country to country with an ease that made some Gentiles uncomfortable. Eventually, these Jews built an effective and profitable international financial network. But the international aspect of this network made some people nervous. It was not long before this discomfort gave birth to theories of international conspiracies.

Since it first appeared, *The Protocols* has been translated into more than a dozen languages; it has been read, discussed, and argued about all over the world, though responsible Christians have spoken out against it. Reputable scholars have discredited it, and the *Times* of London showed that it had been lifted almost word for word from an 1864 fiction story. But nothing has stopped it for long. Early in the twentieth century, *The Protocols*

This was a cover of a popular French edition of *The Protocols of the Elders of Zion*, entitled *Le Peril Juif* ("The Jewish Threat").

spread into Germany. In Austria, a young man named Adolf Hitler read it, absorbed it, and eventually used it as one of his reasons to "justify" genocide.

"The War to End All Wars"

In the summer of 1914, war erupted in Europe. World War I pitted the Central Powers—Germany, Austria-Hungary, and the Ottoman Empire—against the Allies—France, Great Britain, and Russia. This bloody conflict lasted until 1918 and brought warfare to a new and highly destructive level.

No longer did cavalry (mounted soldiers) and infantry (foot soldiers) march onto a battlefield in ordered lines. No longer were swords, muskets, and cannon the chief weapons. This was trench warfare. Soldiers dug foxholes and fired at one another across a line that none of them could see. Airplanes fought for control of the skies. Mustard gas and other chemical weapons killed or disabled thousands. At sea, submarines could torpedo surface vessels without ever coming up for air.

This faceless, machine-age war left millions of soldiers dead and cost billions of dollars. It was supposed to be a "war to make the world safe for democracy" and a "war to end all wars." It achieved neither of these goals.

On November 11, 1918, an armistice (a cease-fire during treaty negotiations) ended the fighting. World War I was over, and the Central Powers had lost. The German leaders who signed the armistice were not the ones who had fought the war. That government had collapsed, leaving the representatives of a newly formed democratic republic—the Weimar Republic—to deal with the Allies. German nationalists labeled these men "November Criminals" and never forgave them for "betraying" the nation.

Anger Born of Humiliation

The Treaty of Versailles, which was signed in 1919, was even more of a blow to German pride. Germany, as an aggressor nation, was required by the treaty to give up 25,000 square miles

(64,750 square kilometers) of annexed territory, to cut its military to no more than 100,000 men, and to pay $33 billion in reparations (payments for war debts).

On the day the treaty was signed, the German newspaper *Deutsche Zeitung* ran this front-page statement:

> *Vengeance! German nation! Today in . . . Versailles the disgraceful treaty is being signed. Do not forget it! . . . Today German honor is being carried to its grave. Do not forget it! The German people will, with unceasing labor, press forward to reconquer the place among the nations to which it is entitled. Then will come vengeance for the shame of 1919.*

With such impassioned opposition, the democratic Weimar Republic was doomed before it even started. It shouldered not only the blame for the Armistice and the Treaty of Versailles but also the anger borne of humiliation. Ensuing power struggles weakened the government, while runaway inflation destroyed the economy. Before the war, four German marks had equaled one U.S. dollar. That exchange rate rose to 191 marks to the dollar by 1922. From there, German currency plunged even more, eventually to virtual worthlessness. By the end of 1923, it took *4 trillion* marks to equal one dollar. With this chaos, Germany was ripe for a new leader who could offer easy answers and a clear way out of the mess.

The young Adolf Hitler had plenty of those easy answers. The November Criminals, he said, were to blame—and so were the Jews. He proposed that Germany follow a new path, one that would lead to the creation of a "Third Reich" ("Third Empire"). This Reich would be based upon nationalism, racism, and the *Führerprinzip* ("Leadership Principle").

The term "Third Reich" most intentionally linked Hitler and his Nazis to German history. The First Reich was ruled by the Holy Roman Empire; the second was ruled in part by Germany's national hero, Prince Otto von Bismarck (1815–1898). The third great empire would be ruled by Hitler.

Upstarts and Rebels

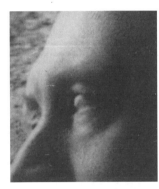

Adolf Hitler did not create the political philosophy of the Nazi Party. Nor did he create the racism and antisemitism on which the Nazis fed. Hitler did, however, bring together a number of political elements in a specific way and at a specific time. His success ultimately led him to the top of an enormously powerful dictatorship that nearly conquered much of Europe.

Hitler: The Early Years

Hitler was born in Austria on April 20, 1889. He was the third child of a customs agent. From the earliest days of his childhood, failure and disappointment marked his life. As a boy, he was a poor student who never earned a School Leaving Certificate—the Austrian equivalent of a diploma. Later, he dreamed of being an artist but failed the entry exam for the Academy of Fine Arts. Then

----
Adolf Hitler stares out from his jail cell in a German prison, 1924. He was arrested after he unsuccessfully tried to take over the German government in a putsch.

An early photo of members of the Nazi Party, 1922. At this point, the group was known primarily as a "marching and chowder club." (Julius Streicher, seated center, later became the publisher of *Der Stürmer*, an antisemitic newspaper.)

he thought of being an architect, but he couldn't qualify for the training.

In 1909, Hitler went to Vienna, the capital of Austria, where he eked out a living working at odd jobs and sleeping in shabby roominghouses. During these aimless years, he began to see the world as a dangerous place, full of traps and plots and secret enemies.

The most obvious enemies, he soon decided, were the Jews. It was at that point in his life that his lifelong dedication to antisemitism began. As he explained in his autobiography *Mein Kampf*, written much later, in 1924, Hitler never forgot his first glimpse of an ultra-Orthodox Jew in the streets of Vienna:

> *I suddenly [saw] an apparition in black caftan and black sidelocks. Is this a Jew? was my first thought. For, to be sure, they had not looked like that [at home]. I observed the man [secretly], but the longer I stared at this foreign face, feature for feature, the more my first question [took] new form: Is this a German?*

In September 1919, Hitler met up with a group in Germany that shared his fears and his strongly antisemitic feelings. At this point, however, the "German Workers' Party" was just a small collection of misfits. The first meeting he attended drew only 25 people to a lecture on economics. Less than a year later, Hitler had become their director of propaganda. The party also changed its name: On April 1, 1920, the German Workers' Party became the National Socialist German Workers' (Nazi) Party.

The Beer Hall Rebellion

On November 8, 1923, Hitler led a detachment of Nazi storm-troopers into a Munich beer hall and proclaimed a putsch—a takeover of the government. Stormtrooper leader Ernst Roehm stationed his men around the hall while Hitler "kidnapped" three state officials at gunpoint and forced them into a back room.

There, he ranted and raved, waving his gun in their faces and demanding that they join his "revolution." After a long, tense evening, the men agreed—or, at least, they pretended to agree. A jubilant Hitler made plans for a march on Munich, the capital of the German state of Bavaria, where he would assume power and place other Nazis in key government positions.

The next morning, some 3,000 Nazis and Nazi sympathizers marched on the Bavarian State Ministry, but the marchers were met in the streets by the Munich police. The clash sooned turned into a shootout in the streets. Hitler turned and ran. Two days later, he was arrested for treason and put in jail.

With the failure in Munich and Hitler behind bars, it appeared as if the Nazi Party had met with a quick collapse. But Hitler had

Hitler (in the trenchcoat) stands with the other chief defendants in the putsch trial, March 1924.

a knack for turning disaster to his own advantage. During his nine months in prison, influenced by writings that spanned the ages, he continued to develop his political and racist ideas. With the help of fellow prisoner Rudolf Hess, he wrote *Mein Kampf* ("My Struggle"), the book that was to become the "bible" of the Nazis' unique form of fascism (a totalitarian political philosophy).

To understand the evolution of Hitler's political beliefs is to understand, in great part, the evolution of his hatred of the Jews. Jewish values clashed head-on with Hitler's Fascist ideals. As scientist Albert Einstein wrote of Judaism:

> *The pursuit of knowledge for its own sake, an almost fanatical love of justice and the desire for personal independence—these are the features of the Jewish tradition which make me thank my stars that I belong to it. Those who are raging today against the ideals of reason and individual liberty and are trying to establish a spiritless state-slavery by brute force rightly see in us [Jews] their irreconcilable foes. History has given us a difficult row to hoe; but so long as we remain devoted servants of truth, justice, and liberty, we shall continue . . . to bring forth fruits which contribute to the ennoblement of the human race.*

The Idea of Race

As part of their evolving plan to deal with the "problem" of the Jews, Hitler and his colleagues expanded upon the destructive theories about the "genetic make-up" of Jews that had emerged in the 1800s. Their theories were based on the idea that Jews were a biologically "inferior race" of people, one that was polluting the "true German" ("Aryan") gene pool. Certainly, the desire to keep Jews from interacting with Gentile society was not new. But, this "biological" basis for doing so was.

To Hitler and the Nazis, Jewishness was both inborn and inescapable. "Without the clearest recognition of the race problem and, with it, of the Jewish question, there will be no rise of the German nation," wrote Hitler in *Mein Kampf*. "The race question not only furnishes the key to world history, but also to human culture as a whole." From such "racist" ideas, however misguided, came a pervasive concept of the "eternal Jew."

Though they did not realize it at the time, Europe's Jews had now entered an era that was far more threatening and dangerous than ever before. With the growing acceptance of Hitler's radical hate-mongering theories would come increasingly more severe attempts at solving the "Jewish problem." But this time, converting and absorbing Jews into the larger society would not be an answer. This time, it would mean much more than barring Jews from professions, marking them, or isolating them. This time, "true Germans"

Franz Eher Nachf. G. m. b. H.
Deutschvölkische Verlagsbuchhandlung
Fernruf 20047 • München • Thierschstraße 15

Postscheck-Konto: Nr. 11340 München
Bank-Konto: Deutsche Hansabank A.-G. München

Kommissionär:
Herr Robert Hoffmann, Leipzig

4½ Jahre Kampf
gegen Lüge, Dummheit und Feigheit
Eine Abrechnung von Adolf Hitler

Leitspruch

„Sie müssen sich gegenseitig wieder achten lernen, der Arbeiter der Stirne den Arbeiter der Faust und umgekehrt. Keiner von beiden bestünde ohne den anderen. Aus ihnen heraus muß sich ein neuer Mensch kristallisieren: Der Mensch des kommenden Deutschen Reiches!"   Adolf Hitler.

Der Eher-Verlag kündigt „Mein Kampf" an. 1924
Die kürzere Fassung des endgültigen Titels ist wesentlich schlagkräftiger!

This advertisement from 1924 used the original title of what became *Mein Kampf*. The original title translated to "4½ Year Struggle."

believed they would have to take much more extreme measures in order to purge themselves once and for all of an entire people.

The Gathering Storm

The Great Depression of the 1930s sent Germany's battle-scarred economy into a deep plunge. By then, Adolf Hitler had become a prominent leader of opposition to the Weimar government. His unique style of fiery and impassioned oratory captivated hundreds of thousands of Germans. In his speeches, Hitler provided Jews as a target, or scapegoat, for "true Germans'" frustration and anger. And his grandiose political ideas gave them an immediate plan of action that they believed would improve their lives.

Public dissatisfaction with the Weimar government expressed itself at the polls in November 1932. When the votes were counted, the Nazi Party had amassed an impressive 34 percent of the vote, which gave the Nazis an influential number of seats in the Reichstag (the German Parliament).

A German police officer walks the streets of Berlin with an SS auxiliary policeman and dog, March 1933. These police forces were often used to suppress political opponents of the Nazi regime.

Riding the wave of that success, Hitler was named chancellor of the German nation on January 30, 1933. He was now the second most powerful man in Germany. Less than 10 years after his failed beer-hall putsch, Hitler was accepting the responsibilities of his new office from none other than the president of Germany himself, Paul von Hindenburg. The Third Reich had begun.

Communists, Traitors, and Fall Guys

As chancellor, Hitler's first goal was to strengthen his power. On February 27, 1933, a purposely set fire at the Reichstag building in Berlin provided the excuse he needed. A man named Marinus van der Lubbe was arrested for the crime. (Many historians, however, believe that the Nazis themselves set the fire and arranged for van der Lubbe to take the blame.)

President von Hindenburg greets Chancellor Hitler at a public ceremony in Berlin, 1934.

The Reichstag building in Berlin is consumed by flames on the night of February 27, 1933.

Van der Lubbe was the perfect fall guy; he was known to love to set fires and was a recognized Communist sympathizer. His alleged involvement was all the Nazis needed to convince the public that Communist revolutionaries threatened Germany and its duly elected government.

Hitler used this threat to convince President von Hindenburg to issue a decree giving the government broad power over the people. This "emergency" order placed restrictions on individuals'

Members of the Nazi Party burn the flag of the Weimar Republic on the streets of Berlin, March 1933.

freedom of speech and rights of assembly and association. The press was muzzled. Homes could be searched and private property could be confiscated by the government without restriction.

With civil liberties officially suspended, the Nazis could attack their enemies. Nazi stormtroopers wearing brown uniforms and hobnailed boots swarmed across Germany, breaking up public meetings, smashing their way into private homes, and beating people senseless in the streets. All over the nation, Communists, Social Democrats, and Jews were arrested without warrant and held without trial. The Nazis also established Germany's first concentration (labor) camp. Named Dachau, the camp was used as a dumping ground for political prisoners.

Consolidation of Power

On March 23, 1933, the Reichstag passed an "enabling law." This gave the Parliament's own law-making powers to Adolf Hitler for a period of four years. In the streets outside, a huge crowd roared its approval as the law transformed the Reichstag into a "rubber-stamp" legislature. It also reduced the aging von Hindenburg to a mere figurehead president.

Hitler promptly put his new power to the test by launching a nationwide boycott of Jewish shops and businesses. Protest from citizens of other nations, especially the United States, was swift and strong. At a massive rally in New York City, outraged Americans threatened a counter-boycott of all German goods.

But Hitler, who had an uncanny ability to gauge public opinion, decided to limit the boycott to a single day: Saturday, April 1, 1933, beginning at 10:00 A.M. Promptly at that time, stormtroopers took up positions outside Jewish shops, and signs went up

Although international reaction was generally weak in 1933, some citizens did speak out against antisemitism. Here, British Jews gather in London to protest Germany's anti-Jewish laws of 1933.

A Nazi stormtrooper stands in front of a Jewish-owned shop in Berlin during the boycott of April 1, 1933.

urging non-Jewish Germans not to enter. For the Nazis, this boycott was fruitful: It rallied the German people, frightened the Jews. And because it was brief, it silenced foreign protest—before effective protest could be mobilized, the whole thing was over.

Emboldened by this success, the Nazis laid the foundation for the "racial" antisemitism that would become the hallmark of their regime. On April 7, the government issued an order dismissing all "non-Aryan" civil servants from their jobs. Historian Martin Gilbert wrote:

> By giving German non-Jews the status of "Aryan," this imaginary concept, based upon nonsensical and discredited theories of "purity of race," Hitler formally divided German citizens into two groups. . . . German cities competed in zealous pursuit of the new "Aryan" ideal. In Frankfurt, on the day of this first "Aryan law," German Jewish teachers were forbidden to teach in the universities, German Jewish actors to perform on the stage, and German Jewish musicians to play in concerts.

A month later, on May 10, the Nazis made yet another strike against "Jewish influence." It happened across the street from the main entrance to Berlin University. A crowd gathered to watch as stormtroopers built a great bonfire. They hauled out boxes full of books—thousands of books by Jewish authors—which they gleefully threw into the flames. Book-burnings such as these would soon become regular frenzies of the Third Reich.

The terrorism mounted as German cities competed with one another to become *Judenrein* ("purified of Jews"). All over the nation, Jews were thrown out of their homes and businesses, beaten, humiliated, even killed.

The government encouraged these displaced people to leave the country. Many of the Jews who were the direct victims of this violence needed little encouragement. In 1933, more than 35,000 German Jews sought refuge in Palestine, Great Britain, Western Europe, Canada, the United States, and other places. By the summer of 1935, the number of Jews emigrating from Germany had reached at least 65,000.

In May 1933, stormtroopers built a great bonfire near Berlin University and destroyed thousands of books by Jewish authors. Top: Nazi students unload "un-German" books for burning. The banner on the truck reads "German students march against the un-German spirit."
Bottom: A huge pile of books burns as spectators rejoice and give the Nazi salute.

Most German Jews, however, did not want to leave. For them, there was no other place to call home. This feeling was understandable—by 1935, Jews had been in Germany for more than a thousand years.

A "Consciousness of Nature"

Under a steady barrage of propaganda and new educational directives, even moderate Germans dredged up a host of half-forgotten prejudices against Jews. Antisemitism now touched every aspect of life, beginning with the public schools. Some prominent educators wrote entire books about how to teach antisemitism in the classroom.

In a book entitled *The Jewish Question—Material and Its Treatment in Schools,* a German teacher explained methods to use with elementary school students:

> *We place two groups of pictures side by side: on the one hand, Nordically [Aryan] classified bodies and faces, sportsman types, Olympic athletes, soldiers, typical officer leaders; on the other hand, we present a group of Jews. . . . Children will feel kinship with the one side, and. . . passionate rejection of the other. . . it is then that the [teacher should]. . . build up. . . this consciousness of the German child's own nature and the complete foreignness of the other [the Jew].*

Antisemitism was taught in all subject areas of the curriculum and in as many different ways as possible. In one third-grade geography class, the teacher told her students that the United States was "deteriorating." The teacher displayed pictures supposedly showing

> *. . . starving men along sidewalks and wharves in American cities. . . . The reactions were written clearly on the faces of the listening boys. A country where such things could be need not be respected, much less feared.*

Ancient Symbol

Despite common belief, the swastika was not created by the Nazi Party. In fact, in parts of Asia, the symbol has been found on artifacts that date to 3,000 years before the Common Era. In Europe, documented uses of swastikas go back to the Bronze Age.

The bent-arm cross icon is usually interpreted as a sun or a fire symbol. On Native American artifacts—particularly those of the Navajo—the symbol is often used to represent the gods of rain and wind. In Norse mythology, however, it is believed to have been a symbol of the hammer of the god of thunder, Thor.

In Austria and Germany, by the twentieth century, the swastika came to be regarded as a peculiarly "Aryan" symbol. This idea led Hitler to incorporate a swastika into the official flag of the Nazi Party. On the flag, a black swastika is centered inside a white circle, which sits on a field of brilliant red.

Hitler addresses the Reichstag.

The teacher had one parting shot:

". . . and the leader of the United States? Who is he?"
"Roosevelt," somebody said.
The teacher's voice got mysterious. "Roosevelt he calls himself. But his real name is Rosenfeldt. What does that show you?"
"He's a Jew," shouted the class.

By August 1935, Hitler and the Nazis were ready to begin implementation of their plans on an even grander scale. In September, the Nazi leadership would convene in the German city of Nuremberg to finalize a collection of wide-reaching laws against all Jews. Known as the Nuremberg Laws, these restrictions would strip Jews of all their rights as citizens.

Without their businesses, jobs, homes, or freedom, Germany's Jews would become panicked and confused. And from there, they would witness the gradual but complete destruction of everything they had once known.

Chronology: 70 C.E.–September 1935

From the Destruction of Jerusalem to Zionism	
70	Jerusalem destroyed by Titus (Roman Empire)
1096	First Crusade
1144	First recorded ritual murder ("blood libel") accusation
1171	Ritual murder charge in Blois, France, leads to the burning alive of entire Jewish community
1215	Pope imposes restrictions on Jews (wearing of badges, "Jews'-hats")
1290	Jews expelled from England
1298	Host desecration charge results in massacre of thousands of Jews in Germany and Austria
1348	Jews blamed for spreading "Black Death" (plague)
1399	First Polish "blood libel"
1480	Spanish Inquisition
1492	Jews expelled from Spain
1500	Beginning of pogroms in Poland
1648	Beginning of Chmielnicki massacres in Russia and Poland
1789	French Revolution
1791	Jews become full citizens in France
1804	Pale of Settlement established in Russia
1812	Jews emancipated in German state of Prussia
1860	Jews emancipated in British Empire
1879	Wilhelm Marr coins term *antisemitism*
1889	Adolf Hitler born in Austria on April 20
1894	Dreyfus Affair in France
1897	First Zionist Congress at Basel, Switzerland

The Twentieth Century	
1903	*The Protocols of the Elders of Zion* published
1914	World War I begins
Oct. 24, 1917	Communist Revolution in Russia
Nov. 11, 1918	Armistice ends World War I
June 28, 1919	Treaty of Versailles is signed
Apr. 1, 1920	The German Workers' Party changes its name to National Socialist German Workers' (Nazi) Party
Nov. 8, 1923	Adolf Hitler's beer-hall putsch
1929	Beginning of Great Depression worldwide
Jan. 30, 1933	Hitler becomes chancellor of Germany
Feb. 27, 1933	Reichstag fire
Feb. 28, 1933	Presidential decree gives Hitler emergency powers
Mar. 24, 1933	Reichstag hands over its powers to Adolf Hitler
Apr. 1, 1933	National boycott against Jewish shops
Apr. 7, 1933	Jews excluded from government employment
May 10, 1933	Book burning at University of Berlin
Aug. 2, 1934	Germany's president von Hindenburg dies; Hitler becomes *Führer*
Sept. 15, 1935	Nuremberg Laws are passed; rights and protections for Jews in Germany severely curtailed

CHRONOLOGY OF THE HOLOCAUST: 1933–1945

1933

January 30
Adolf Hitler becomes chancellor of Germany

February 28
Nazis declare emergency after Reichstag fire; consolidate power

March 22
Nazis open first concentration camp: Dachau

May 10
Public book burnings target works by Jews and opponents of the Nazis

July 14
Nazi Party established as one and only legal party in Germany

1934

January 26
German–Polish non-aggression pact signed

1935

September 15
Nuremberg Laws passed

1936

March
Germany occupies Rhineland, flouting the Versailles Treaty

August
Olympic Games held in Berlin

1938

November 9–10
Kristallnacht: long-planned pogrom explodes across "Greater Germany"

September 29
Munich Conference: appeasement; Allies grant Germany Sudetenland (part of Czechoslovakia)

July 6–13
Evian Conference: refugee policies

March 13
Anschluss: annexation of Austria

1937

September 7
Hitler declares end of the Versailles Treaty

1939

May
British White Paper: Jewish emigration to Palestine limited

August 23
Soviet–German non-aggression pact signed

September 1
Germany invades Poland; Poland falls within a month

September 2
Great Britain and France declare war on Germany

September 17
Red (Soviet) Army invades eastern Poland

October 8
First ghetto established in Poland

1941

June 22
Operation Barbarossa: invasion of the Soviet Union; German war on two fronts

March 24
Germany invades North Africa

1940

October 16
Order for creation of Warsaw ghetto

April 27
Heinrich Himmler orders creation of Auschwitz concentration camp; established May 20

Spring
Germany conquers Denmark, Norway, Belgium, Luxembourg, Holland, and France (occupies northern part)

February 12
Deportation of Jews from Germany to occupied Poland begins

July 31
Reinhard Heydrich appointed to implement "Final Solution": extermination of European Jewry

December 7
Japan attacks Pearl Harbor

December 11
Germany and Italy declare war on the United States

1942

January 20
Wannsee Conference: coordination of "Final Solution"

Spring–Summer
Liquidation of Polish ghettos; deportation of Jews to extermination camps

November 19–20
Soviet Army counterattacks at Stalingrad

1944

May–July
Deportation of Hungarian Jews: 437,402 sent to Auschwitz

June 6
D-Day: Allies invade Normandy

July
Soviet troops liberate Majdanek camp in Poland

October 2
Danes rescue more than 7,200 Jews from Nazis

June 11
Heinrich Himmler orders liquidation of all ghettos in Poland and the Soviet Union

April 19–May 16
Warsaw ghetto uprising

April 19
Bermuda Conference: fruitless discussion of rescue of Jewish victims of Nazis; liquidation of Warsaw ghetto begins

1943

January 18–21
Major act of resistance in Warsaw ghetto

January 27
Soviet troops liberate Auschwitz–Birkenau

April–May
Allies liberate Buchenwald, Bergen-Belsen, Dachau, Mauthausen, and Theresienstadt concentration camps

April 30
Hitler commits suicide

May 7
Germany surrenders unconditionally to Allies

May 8
V-E Day: Victory in Europe

November
Nuremberg Trials begin

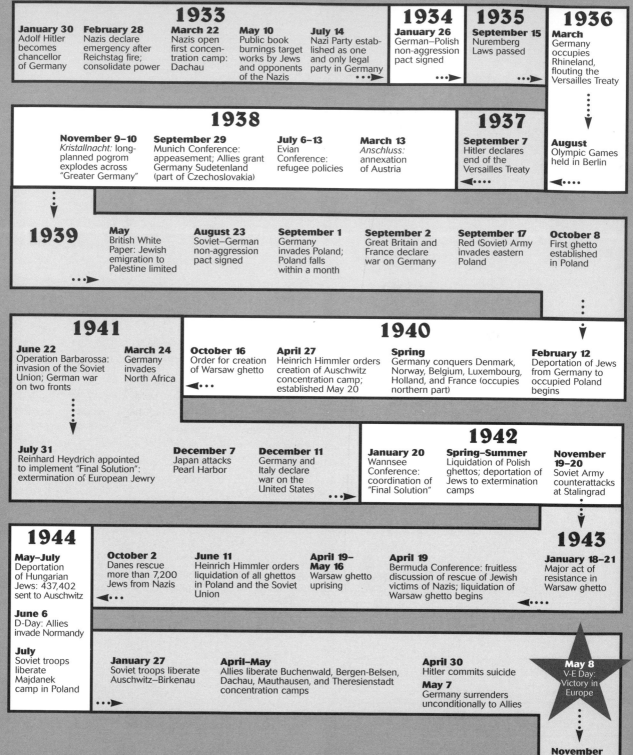

Glossary

Anti-Semite A person who hates Jews.

Antisemitism Hatred of Jews.

Armistice The stopping of war hostilities—a cease-fire—until a peace treaty is signed.

Ashkenazi A term for the Jews who dispersed to Central and Eastern Europe and established many settlements there.

Blood Libel The belief that Jews killed Christian children in order to use their blood in rituals.

Bubonic Plague A highly infectious disease that killed an estimated 25 million people in the mid- to late 1300s. *Also called the Black Death.*

Civil Liberties Personal freedoms guaranteed to citizens of a country, including rights such as freedom of speech, the right to assembly, and freedom from illegal search.

Coalition Two or more groups—such as political parties—that work together in order to pursue a common goal.

Collective Bargaining A negotiation technique in which large groups of workers select people to represent them in labor-management discussions.

Communism A political, social, and economic ideology that aims for a classless society. German Communists were the first opponents of the Nazis.

Concentration Camps Labor camps set up by the Nazis to house political prisoners or people they considered to be "undesirable." Prisoners were made to work like slaves and many died as a result of starvation, disease, or beatings. *Also called work camps, work centers, and prison camps.*

Conversos The Spanish term for Jews who converted to Christianity.

Crusades A series of campaigns in the Middle Ages to capture the Holy Land of Palestine.

Desecrate To treat a holy object disrespectfully.

Diaspora A dispersion of Jews to other lands.

Extermination Camps Death camps built by the Nazis in German-occupied Poland for the sole purpose of killing "enemies" of the Third Reich. The most common method of murder used at these camps was poisonous gas. The victims' bodies were usually burned in ovens in the crematoria. The six extermination camps were Auschwitz-Birkenau, Belzec, Chelmno, Majdanek, Sobibór, and Treblinka. *Also called killing centers.*

Final Solution The Nazis' plan to exterminate the Jews of Europe.

Führer A German word meaning "leader." It was used to refer to Adolf Hitler, dictator of Germany from 1933 to 1945 and head of the Nazi Party.

Fuehrerprinzip Hitler's "leadership principle."

Genocide The deliberate and systematic murder of an entire race, class, or large group of people.

Gentile A non-Jewish person.

Ghetto A part of a city, sometimes sealed off, where Jews were forced to live, apart from other people.

Hebrews An early name for the Jews.

Heretic A person who holds religious views that are different from established doctrine or beliefs.

Holocaust A term for the state-sponsored, systematic persecution and annihilation of European Jewry by Nazi Germany and its collaborators between 1933 and 1945. While Jews were the primary victims, with approximately 6 million murdered, many other groups were targeted, including Romani (Gypsies), the disabled, Soviet prisoners of war, political dissidents, Jehovah's Witnesses, and male homosexuals. It is believed that perhaps 4 million non-Jews were killed under the Nazi regime.

Host Desecration The belief that Jews desecrated the Host used in Christian Holy Communion.

Infidel To the Christians of the Middle Ages, a person who did not believe in the doctrines of the Christian faith or who practiced another religion, such as a Jew or Muslim (follower of Islam).

Islam A monotheistic religion founded by the Prophet Muhammad in the 600s C.E.

Jews People who belong to the religion of Judaism.

Judaism The oldest surviving monotheistic religion, founded by Abraham circa 1800-1600 C.E.

Judenrein A term meaning "purified of Jews," Hitler's goal for Germany.

Lebensraum A German term for "living space" to accommodate what the Nazis called the "master race" of Aryan people.

Marranos Spanish Jews who claimed to have converted to Christianity but who continued to practice Judaism in secret.

Mein Kampf In English, "My Struggle," a book written by Adolf Hitler while he was in prison in 1924, in which he outlined his plans for Germany.

Monotheism The worship of a singular God. Judaism was the first monotheistic religion.

Nazi A member of the Nazi Party or something associated with the party, such as "Nazi government."

Nazi Party Short for the National Socialist German Workers Party. Founded in 1919, the party became a potent political force under Hitler's leadership.

Nuremberg Laws "Reich Citizenship Laws," passed on September 15, 1935. These sweeping laws specified the qualifications for German citizenship and excluded from citizenship persons of Jewish ancestry.

Pale of Settlement A region of Czarist Russia to which all Jews in Russian lands were forced to move beginning in 1772.

Palestine A region in the Middle East, part of which is now known as Israel. Palestine was controlled by the British government from 1922 to 1948.

Pogroms Organized, mass attacks on a group of people.

Propaganda The deliberate spreading of ideas, information or rumors—often false—for the purpose of helping or injuring a cause, organization, or person.

Passover A holiday celebrating the Jews' Exodus from slavery in Egypt to freedom.

Putsch The sudden takeover of a government; a coup.

Rabbi In Judaism, a leader or teacher.

Reformation A religious movement begun in 1517 by Martin Luther, the founder of Protestantism.

Reichstag The German Parliament.

SA From the German term *Sturmabteilungen*, meaning "stormtroopers." The SA were Nazi soldiers. Also called *brown-shirts*.

Sephardic A term for the Jews who followed the spread of Islam to Spain and other lands. Well-educated urban-dwellers, they developed a rich religious tradition.

Shtetls Jewish villages.

Spanish Inquisition An attempt by the Spanish state to unify the country by ensuring that *conversos* were not secretly practicing Judaism.

Swastika An ancient design that the Nazis adapted for their party symbol.

Star of David The six-pointed star that is a symbol of Judaism.

Synagogue The Jews' house of worship.

Third Reich Reich means "empire." In German history, the First Reich lasted from 962 until 1806, the second from 1871 to 1918. In the early 1920s, Hitler began using the term "Third Reich" to describe his own empire, which lasted from 1933 until 1945.

Torah The first five books of the Hebrew Bible.

Trade Union A workers' organization that seeks better wages, working conditions, and benefits through collective bargaining.

Treaty of Versailles The 1919 peace treaty that ended World War I and outlined the terms of surrender for Germany and the Axis powers.

Yiddish The vibrant, everyday language spoken in the *shtetls*.

Source Notes

Introduction:

Page 10: "First they came...." Quoted in Michael Berenbaum. *The World Must Know*. Boston: Little, Brown, 1993, p. 41.

Page 11: "...a racially pure...." Adolf Hitler. *Mein Kampf* ("My Struggle").

Page 11–12: "Jewry...has special...." Adolf Hitler. *Zweites Buch* ("Secret Book"). 1928.

Page 13: "...settle as immigrants...." Bernard Lazare. *Antisemitism: Its History and Causes*. Lincoln, NE: University of Nebraska Press; Bison Books, 1995, p. 19.

Page 13: "The War Against...." Berenbaum, p. 2.

Chapter 1:

Page 16: "...was not 'a god,' but God...." Robert M. Seltzer. *Jewish People, Jewish Thought: The Jewish Experience in History*. New York: Macmillan, 1980, p. 37.

Page 16: "Not only did [God] say...." Lazare, pp. 9–10.

Page 17: "The Jews and their Scripture...." Seltzer, p. 164.

Page 19: "A remark attributed...." Seltzer, p. 175.

Chapter 2:

Page 25: "They put a rope around his neck and dragged him...." "Mainz Anonymous" manuscript quoted in Robert Chazan. *In the Year 1096.... The First Crusade & the Jews*. Philadelphia, PA: The Jewish Publication Society, 1996, pp. 32–33.

Page 26: "From the time of the first crusade...." Norman Cohn. *Warrant for Genocide: The Myth of the Jewish World Conspiracy and the Protocols of the Elders of Zion*. London: Serif, 1996, p. 26.

Page 28: "...the Jews...stole a child called Hugh...." Quoted in Nathan Ausubel. *The Book of Jewish Knowledge*. New York: Crown, 1964, p. 370.

Page 32: "[The Catholics] have dealt...." Max Dimont. *Jews, God and History*. New York: Simon & Schuster, 1962, p. 227.

Pages 32–33: "Set their synagogues...." Quoted in Ausubel, p. 313.

Chapter 3:

Page 39: "Yiddish uses the letters...." Leo Rosten. *Hooray for Yiddish!* New York: Simon & Schuster, 1982, pp. 10–11.

Page 42: "Until 1930, the sole mode...." Ellen Livingston. *Tradition and Modernism in the Shtetl Aisheshuk, 1919–1939*. Princeton, NJ: Princeton University Press, 1986, pp. 19–20.

Page 43: "We were children...." Livingston, p. 74.

Page 44–45: "The Dreyfus case [is] more than a judicial error...." Quoted in Alex Bein. *Theodore Herzl*. London: East and West Library, 1957, pp. 115–116.

Page 45: "...to create for...." Quoted in Dimont, p. 398.

Chapter 4:

Page 51: "Vengeance! German nation...." Koppel Pinson. *Modern Germany*. New York: Macmillan Co, 1954, p. 398.

Chapter 5:

Page 54: "I suddenly [saw]...." Hitler, *Mein Kampf*.

Page 56: "The pursuit of knowledge for its own sake..." Albert Einstein. *Ideas and Opinions*. New York: Crown, 1954, p. 185.

Page 56: "Without the clearest recognition of the race problem..." Adolf Hitler. *Mein Kampf*. Quoted in George L. Mosse. *Nazi Culture: A Documentary History*. New York: Schocken Books, 1981, p. 9.

Chapter 6:

Page 65: "By giving German...." Martin Gilbert. *The History of the Jews of Europe During the Second World War*. New York: Holt, Rinehart & Winston, 1985, p. 36.

Page 67: "We place two groups of pictures side by side...." Quoted in Margot Stern Strom and William S. Parsons. *Facing History and Ourselves: Holocaust and Human Behavior*. Watertown, MA: Intentional Educations, 1982, p. 178.

Page 67: "...starving men in American...." Quoted in Strom and Parsons, p. 176.

Page 69: "...and the leader...." Quoted in Strom and Parsons, p. 176.

Further Reading

Linda Jacobs Altman. *Genocide: The Systematic Killing of a People.* Springfield, NJ: Enslow Publishers, 1995. Contains an overview chapter on the Holocaust, with material on antisemitism and other forms of racism.

Alicia Appleman-Jurman. *Alicia: My Story.* New York: Bantam Books, 1988. The Holocaust memories of a thirteen-year-old member of the Jewish underground.

Michael Berenbaum. *The World Must Know.* Boston: Little, Brown, 1993.

Anne Frank. *Anne Frank: The Diary of a Young Girl.* Garden City, NY: Doubleday, 1967.

Ellen Frankel. *The Classic Tales: 4,000 Years of Jewish Lore.* New York: Jason Aronson, Inc, 1989.

Eileen Heyes. *Adolf Hitler.* Brookfield, CT: Millbrook Press.

Eileen Heyes. *Children of the Swastika: The Hitler Youth.* Brookfield, CT: Millbrook Press.

Johanna Hurwitz. *Anne Frank: Life in Hiding.* Philadelphia: The Jewish Publication Society.

Kerry M. Olitzky and Ronald H. Isaacs. *A Glossary of Jewish Life.* Northvale, NJ: Jason Aronson, 1996.

Steven Otfinoski. *Joseph Stalin: Russia's Last Czar.* Brookfield, CT: Millbrook Press.

Robert M. Seltzer. *Jewish People, Jewish Thought: The Jewish Experience in History.* New York: Macmillan, 1980.

William L. Shirer. *The Rise and Fall of Adolf Hitler.* New York: Scholastic Book Services, 1961.

Illse-Margret Vogel. *Bad Times, Good Friends: A Personal Memoir.* San Diego, CA: Harcourt Brace Jovanovich Publishers, 1992.

Bibliography

Nathan Ausubel. *The Book of Jewish Knowledge*. New York: Crown, 1964.

Alex Bein. *Theodore Herzl*. London: East and West Library, 1957.

Michael Berenbaum. *The World Must Know*. Boston: Little, Brown, 1993.

Norman F. Cantor. *Medieval History: the Life and Death of a Civilization*. 2nd ed. New York: Macmillan, 1969.

Robert Chazan. *In the Year 1096… The First Crusade & the Jews*. Philadelphia: The Jewish Publication Society, 1996.

Norman Cohn. *Warrant for Genocide: The Myth of the Jewish World Conspiracy and the Protocols of the Elders of Zion*, 1967; London: Serif, 1996.

Max I. Dimont. *Jews, God and History*. New York: Charles Scribners' Sons; Signet, 1962.

Albert Einstein. *Ideas and Opinions*. New York: Crown, 1954.

Martin Gilbert. *The History of the Jews of Europe During the Second World War*. New York: Holt, Rinehart & Winston, 1985.

Calvin Goldscheider and Alan S. Zuckerman. *The Transformation of the Jews*. Chicago: University of Chicago Press, 1984.

Celia S. Heller. *On the Edge of Destruction: Jews of Poland Between the Two World Wars*. New York: Schocken Books, 1980.

Arthur Koestler. *The Thirteenth Tribe*. New York: Random House, 1978.

Bernard Lazare. *Antisemitism: Its History and Causes*. Lincoln, NE: University of Nebraska Press; Bison Books, 1995.

Ezckicl Lcikin. *The Beilis Transcripts: The Anti-Semitic Trial that Shook the World*. Northvale, NJ: Jason Aronson, 1993.

Ellen Livingston. *Tradition and Modernism in the Shtetl Aisheshuk, 1919–1939*. Princeton, NJ: Princeton University Press, 1986.

George L. Mosse. *Nazi Culture: A Documentary History*. New York: Schocken Books, 1981.

Koppel Pinson. *Modern Germany*. New York: Macmillan, 1954.

Robert N. Proctor. *Racial Hygiene: Medicine Under the Nazis*. Cambridge, MA: Harvard University Press, 1988.

James Bruce Ross and Mary Martin McLaughlin, eds. *The Portable Medieval Reader*. New York: Viking Press, 1964.

Robert M. Seltzer. *Jewish People, Jewish Thought: The Jewish Experience in History*. New York: Macmillan, 1980.

William L. Shirer. *The Rise and Fall of the Third Reich.* New York: Simon & Schuster, 1959; Fawcett World Library, 1962.

Margot Stern Strom and William S. Parsons. *Facing History and Ourselves: Holocaust and Human Behavior.* Watertown, MA: Intentional Educations, 1982.

Germania, Tacitus. *The Agricola and Germany of Tacitus.* Trans. by A.J. Church and W.J. Brodribb. London: Macmillan, 1885, excerpted in Norman F. Cantor, editor. *The Medieval World: 300-1300.* New York: Macmillan, 1963.

Leo Trepp. *A History of the Jewish Experience.* New York: Berman House, 1973.

John Weiss. *Ideology of Death: Why the Holocaust Happened in Germany.* Chicago: Ivan R. Dee, 1996.

Index

Photo Credits
Cover: Scala/Art Resource, NY; pages 8, 9, 63: Main Commission for the Investigation of Nazi Crimes, courtesy of USHMM Photo Archives; pages 10, 46, 47, 64: National Archives; pages 14, 15, 18, 20, 21, 25, 30, 33, 34, 35, 40, 45: North Wind Picture Archives; pages 27, 44, 66 (top): Courtesy of USHMM Photo Archives; page 43: Ita Benhaiem, courtesy of USHMM Photo Archives; page 49: Wiener Library, courtesy of USHMM Photo Archives; pages 52, 53, 55, 58, 59, 60, 62, 66 (bottom): Bundesarchiv, courtesy of USHMM Photo Archives; page 54: Joanne Schartow, courtesy of USHMM Photo Archives; page 57: Library of Congress, courtesy of USHMM Photo Archives; page 61: Bildarchiv Preussischer Kulturbesitz, courtesy of USHMM Photo Archives; page 68: Rijksinstituut vor Oorlogsdocumentatie, courtesy of USHMM Photo Archives.

Maps and graphs ©Blackbirch Press, Inc.

DATE DUE

Staff 14			

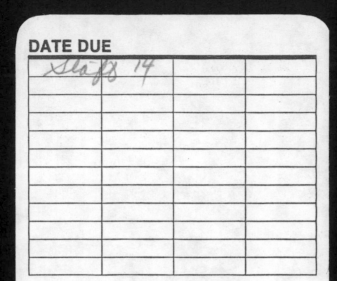